The Essence of the Word of God Illustrated

Written by Ada Onwukeme

Illustrated by Elena Paun

Serendipity Press, Jos

"…His Excellence is over Serendipity Press…" Ps.68:34b

The Essence of the Word of God Illustrated

Published by Serendipity Press, Jos

www.adaonwukeme.com

Copyright © 2020 by Serendipity Press, Jos

All rights reserved. No portion of this book may be reproduced in any form or any means without the written permission of the publisher, with the exception of brief excerpts in reviews.

As a partridge that broods but does not hatch, so is he who gets riches, but not by right; it will leave him in the midst of his days, and at the end be a fool. Jeremiah 17:11

The Essence of The Word God Illustrated

Summary: Thirteen everyday objects depicts the relevance of the Word of God in one's life. The reader goes away with an understanding, clarity and a desire to read the Word of God.

ISBN 10-digit 978-36057-4-7
ISBN 13-digit 978-97836057-4-9

APPRECIATION

LORD God Almighty, thank You for Your help to publish this book. I am thankful to all the wonderful people who me helped put this book together: Fr. Tom Francis, Mrs. Nkechi Okereke and Timothy Johnson.

DEDICATION

This book is dedicated to my awesome parents
Mazi Edmund N. & Mrs. Grace N. U. Onwukeme

"All Scripture is inspired by God and is useful for teaching, for refutation, for correction, and for training in righteousness, so that one who belongs to God may be competent, equipped for every good work. 2 Timothy 3:16-17

Napoleon wrote, "The Bible is no mere book, but a Living Creature, with a power that conquers all that oppose it."

George Washington said, "It is impossible to rightly govern the world without God and the Bible."

Hi, my name is Udo! Last year when school was out, my parents sent me to spend my holidays with my grandparents. They live in our ancestral home in Aro-Ndizuogu.

Every day after the evening meal was over, I sat beside grandpa and grandma while they told me fascinating stories. Some were folktales, some were from their own lives. Never was there a night without a story. The stories were captivating, and enchanting.

However, some were sobering, like the one grandma told me the night before I went back to my parents. It made me think, and long to learn to read so I could read Bible stories by myself.

This particular evening, the night air was cool, crisp, and clear. The wind was rustling through the trees making a whispering sound. The moonlight flooded the compound, and made the stories more enchanting. Truly, I was enthralled. It was a perfect night for stories! As I sat down beside grandma for the night's story, my eyes caught sight of a beautiful big book.

"Grandma, what is the name of this big book?" I asked. "My dear it is the Holy Bible." Grandma replied. "What is it about?" I persisted. "Ha, my son, it is the Holy Bible. It is the Word of God to us." She answered. "What good is it to us, grandma?" I asked, more curious than ever.

She paused for few seconds looking straight ahead; she stood up and went into the bedroom. She came back with a bag. I thought she had wanted to avoid my question. As I was thinking it over, she cleared her throat.

She dipped her hand inside the bag, and brought out a picture of bread. With the picture of bread in her hand, she said,

BREAD

"THE WORD OF GOD IS LIKE…BREAD."

"My son, as we eat bread to give us strength and energy, so it is with the Word of God. If we do not eat for a day, we will be weak to do physical activity. So also, is the Word of God. As we read and think about it, it gives us spiritual and moral strength to overcome temptations and endure trials.

John 6:51 – "I am the living bread which came down from heaven. If anyone eats of this bread, he will live forever; and the bread that I shall give is My flesh, which I shall give for the life of the world." (Isaiah 55:1-3; John 6:48-58, 61-63)

Next, she brought out a picture of fire, and she said,

Fire

"THE WORD OF GOD IS LIKE...FIRE."

"As fire burns up dry leaves, grass, and trash in dumps, so does the Word of God help burn up undesirable desires, behaviors, and attitudes in our lives."

"Jeremiah 23:29A – "Is not My Word like a fire?" says the LORD..."

Next, she brought out a picture of a hammer, and she said,

Hammer

"THE WORD OF GOD IS LIKE... a HAMMER."

"As a hammer is used to break rocks, so the Word of God helps break stony hearts, and our bad attitudes."

Jeremiah 23:29B - "Is not My word...like a hammer that breaks the rock in pieces?

Next, she brought out a picture of a lamp, and she said,

Lamp

"THE WORD OF GOD IS LIKE... a LAMP."

As a lamp lights up a street in the dark, so that we do not run into a ditch or tree, so does the Word of God light up our path in life. It gives us wisdom to choose right from wrong."

Psalm 119:105A – "Your Word is a lamp to my feet..." (Prov.6:23A)

Next, she brought out a picture of medicine, and she said,

Medicine

"THE WORD OF GOD IS LIKE...MEDICINE."

"As medicine is used to ease pain in our body, and to cure diseases. So is the Word of God as we read, and apply it daily in our lives. It heals the aches in our spirit, soul, (heart) and body. It cures the root cause of our misery."

Psalm 107:20 - "He sent His Word and healed them, and delivered them from their destructions." (Rev.12:11; Isa.53:5; 1Pet.2:24)

Next, my grandma brought out a picture of a mirror, and she said,

Mirror

"THE WORD OF GOD IS LIKE...a MIRROR."

"We use a mirror to see if our face is clean. If we see any dirt on our face, we wipe it off. So is the Word of God. It helps us to make sure our attitudes, and behavior are good.

James 1:23-25 - "For if anyone is a hearer of the Word and not a doer, he is like a man observing his natural face in a mirror; For he observes himself, goes away, and immediately forgets what kind of man he was. But he who looks into the perfect law of liberty and continues in it, and is not a forgetful hearer but a doer of the word, this one will be blessed in what he does."

Next, she brought out a picture of milk, and she said,

Milk

"THE WORD OF GOD IS LIKE...MILK"

"As babies drink milk to grow and stay healthy, so it is with the Word of God. As we read, and live it out we grow closer to God."

1Peter 2:2 - "As newborn babes, desire the pure milk of the word, that you may grow thereby." (1Corin.3:2)

Next, she brought out a picture of a seed, and she said,

Seed

"THE WORD OF GOD IS LIKE...a SEED"

"As a seed germinates, grows and bears fruit for us to eat. So is the Word of God which we read helps us to behave well, people want to copy us. It gladdens God's Heart.

1Peter 1:23 - "Having been born again, not of corruptible seed but incorruptible, through the word of God which lives and abides forever." (Matt.13:3-8, 32)

Next, she brought out a picture of a sword, and she said,

Sword

"THE WORD OF GOD IS LIKE...a SWORD"

"As the warriors of old used swords to defend their towns and villages. So it is with the Word of God. The Word of God helps us to fight the devil as Jesus did when He was tempted in the wilderness."

Ephesians 6:17 – "And take the helmet of salvation, and the sword of the Spirit, which is the word of God." (Matt.4:4, Rev.12:11)

Next, she brought out a picture of water filling a bathtub, and she said,

Water

"THE WORD OF GOD IS LIKE...WATER"

"As we use water to bath to keep us clean, so do we need the Word of God to keep us clean."

Ephesians 5:26 – "That He [Jesus Christ] might sanctify and cleanse her with the washing of water by the word."

Also

"As we drink water to quench our thirst. So do we need the Word of God to satisfy our soul. As we read the Word of God it gives us life, strengthens, and fortifies our soul."

John 7:37b – "If anyone thirsts, let him come to Me and drink. (Ps.119:9; John 17:17, 4:14; Isa.55:1-2)

Next, she brought out a picture of soap, and she said,

Soap

"THE WORD OF GOD IS LIKE... a SOAP"

"As soap is used to clean our bodies. So will God use His Word to keep us clean."

Malachi 3:2B, 3 - "But who can endure the day of His coming? And who can stand when He appears? For He is like...fuller's soap. ...He will purify the sons of Levi, and purge them as gold and silver, that they may offer to the LORD an offering in righteousness."

Next, she brought out a picture of a table knife, she said,

Table Knife

"THE WORD OF GOD IS LIKE… a TABLE KNIFE"

As we use the table knife to cut open a fruit to eat the edible part to nourish our body to stay healthy, we throw away the inedible part, so the Word of God. It helps us see the thoughts, the intentions, the motives of our hearts thereby it helps us to walk in godly ways."

Hebrews 4:12 - "For the Word of God is living and powerful, and sharper than any two-edged sword (table knife), piercing even to the division of soul and spirit, and of joints and marrow, and is a discerner of the thoughts and intents of heart."

Next, she brought our new house.

NEW HOUSE

"THE WORD OF GOD IS LIKE... a NEW HOUSE"

"As we renovated and fixed the old house and it became a new house, so the Word of God. When we believe in Jesus Christ, He forgives us and cleans us of things we did which did not make Him happy. He makes old things pass away and makes us a new person. He forgets those old things"

2 Corinthians 5:17 "So whoever is in Christ Jesus is a new creation: the old things have passed away; behold, new things have come."

Grandma finished. I thanked my grandma for a wonderful explanation of what the word of God is like. She thanked God for His Word.

As she walked with me into my room, she said to me, "Udo, you know what? God's Word is like a light that brightens a dark room so we do not stumble. It helps us to know the right choice to make. The right choice may make us loose our friends but we will be at peace with God."

"A wrong choice will bring us happiness for the moment with friends but leave us bitter, with heartaches and scars for years to come." With this she tucked me into bed and kissed my forehead, "Goodnight my love," she said, and left the room.

"...And the law is light; reproofs of instructions are the way of life." Prov. 6:23

www.ingramcontent.com/pod-product-compliance
Lightning Source LLC
LaVergne TN
LVHW070604070526
838199LV00012B/484